MW01152611

HOOVER DAM

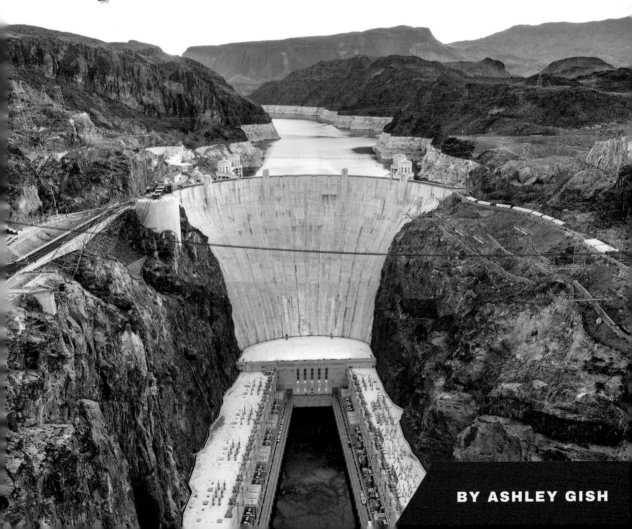

BY ASHLEY GISH

Apex is distributed by North Star Editions:
sales@northstareditions.com | 888-417-0195

Produced for Apex by Red Line Editorial.

Photographs ©: Shutterstock Images, cover, 1, 4–5, 7, 8–9, 10–11, 21, 22–23, 24–25, 26, 27, 29; iStockphoto, 6, 14; National Archives, 12; Ben D. Glaha/Library of Congress, 15, 16–17, 18, 19; Library of Congress, 20

Library of Congress Control Number: 2023910871

ISBN
978-1-63738-750-4 (hardcover)
978-1-63738-793-1 (paperback)
978-1-63738-877-8 (ebook pdf)
978-1-63738-836-5 (hosted ebook)

Printed in the United States of America
Mankato, MN
012024

NOTE TO PARENTS AND EDUCATORS

Apex books are designed to build literacy skills in striving readers. Exciting, high-interest content attracts and holds readers' attention. The text is carefully leveled to allow students to achieve success quickly. Additional features, such as bolded glossary words for difficult terms, help build comprehension.

TABLE OF CONTENTS

CHAPTER 1

DESERT DRIVE

A family drives through the desert. Soon, they reach the Black Canyon. The Colorado River rushes far below. It flows out of Hoover Dam.

The Black Canyon is between Arizona and Nevada.

Hoover Dam stretches 1,244 feet (379 m) across the canyon.

The family explores the dam. They walk on top of the massive concrete structure. The dam is 726 feet (221 m) high.

TALL TOURS

Hoover Dam offers many tours. Visitors can enjoy the observation deck or learn about the **power generators**. They can also see tunnels inside the dam.

About seven million people visit Hoover Dam each year.

Water falls 500 feet (150 m) through pipes to the bottom of the dam.

On one side, the family sees Lake Mead. Four towers jut out of the lake. They let water into the dam. On the other side, the Colorado River flows out.

FAST FACT

Water flows up to 120 miles per hour (190 km/h) through the dam's **spillway** tunnels.

CHAPTER 2

RUSHING RIVER

n the late 1800s, the United States began making plans for the Colorado River. People wanted to use its water. But the river's level varied. Sometimes it flooded. Other times it was too low.

Melted snow from the Rocky Mountains feeds the Colorado River.

In 1918, an **engineer** suggested a dam. It would hold back floodwater. Then, small amounts could be released for farmers year-round.

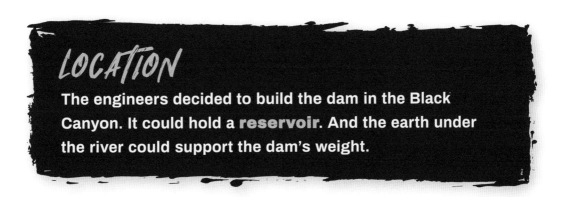

LOCATION

The engineers decided to build the dam in the Black Canyon. It could hold a **reservoir**. And the earth under the river could support the dam's weight.

◀ The area around the Black Canyon is very hot and dry.

The dam was designed with a curved shape. Water would press the dam against the canyon walls. That would make it stronger.

The design used for Hoover Dam is called an arch-gravity dam.

More than 4,000 workers moved to Boulder City to work on Hoover Dam.

FAST FACT

Boulder City, Nevada, was founded in 1931. Dam workers and their families lived there.

CHAPTER 3

CONSTRUCTION

Workers began building Hoover Dam in 1931. They dug tunnels into the canyon walls. The Colorado River flowed through them. That kept the construction site dry.

Huge tunnels redirected the river's flow. They were
56 feet (17 m) tall.

Next, workers smoothed the canyon walls. They used **jackhammers** and explosives. These tools helped remove loose rocks.

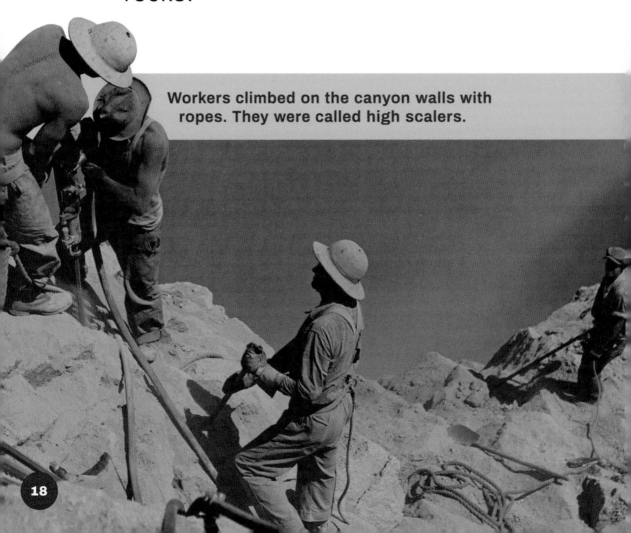

Workers climbed on the canyon walls with ropes. They were called high scalers.

Each intake tower is 395 feet (120 m) tall.

The dam is made of more than 200 concrete blocks.

Then, workers poured huge blocks of concrete. They ran pipes through the blocks. River water flowed through. It cooled and hardened the concrete. Next, new blocks went on top.

MAKING ENERGY

Hoover Dam uses **turbines** to create electricity. Water flows in through the intake towers. The water spins the turbines. The spinning makes energy. Then, the water flows out.

Hoover Dam has 17 water turbines.

CHAPTER 4

IMPACT

Hoover Dam was completed in 1936. Lake Mead became the largest reservoir in the United States. Today, millions of people visit the lake each year.

Lake Mead began filling in 1934. In 1937, it reached 1,045 feet (319 m) deep.

The dam helped farmers.
They could water crops
all year. It helped **irrigate**
more than 1.5 million acres
(610,000 hectares) of farmland.

The Colorado River Aqueduct transports water 242 miles (389 km).

FAST FACT

Aqueducts direct water away from the Colorado River. The water goes to farms and houses.

Hoover Dam also supplied electricity to many people. It helped nearby cities grow. The dam remains important to US states in the Southwest.

Hoover Dam helps power three different states. Energy from the dam reaches 500,000 homes each year.

From 2000 to 2020, water levels at Lake Mead dropped 170 feet (52 m). Lighter rock shows where water used to be.

DEAD POOL

By 2022, Lake Mead's water levels dropped to 1,040 feet (317 m). At 895 feet (273 m), water would stop flowing past the dam. That's called a dead pool. The dam would stop making power.

COMPREHENSION QUESTIONS

Write your answers on a separate piece of paper.

1. Write a few sentences describing how Hoover Dam was built.

2. Which part of Hoover Dam would you most like to tour? Why?

3. What year was Boulder City, Nevada, founded?

   A. 1918

   B. 1931

   C. 1936

4. How long did it take to build the Hoover Dam?

   A. one year

   B. five years

   C. six years

5. What does **massive** mean in this book?

*They walk on top of the **massive** concrete structure. The dam is 726 feet (221 m) high.*

    A. very skinny

    B. very weak

    C. very large

6. What does **varied** mean in this book?

*But the river's level **varied**. Sometimes it flooded. Other times it was too low.*

    A. changed

    B. stopped

    C. heated

Answer key on page 32.

GLOSSARY

aqueducts
Systems that carry water.

engineer
A person who uses math and science to solve problems.

intake
A structure that lets something in.

irrigate
To supply crops with water to help them grow.

jackhammers
Powered drills or hammers used to break rock or pavement.

power generators
Machines that turn energy from motion into electricity.

reservoir
A human-made lake that stores water.

spillway
A passage where water runs over, through, or around a dam.

turbines
Machines that create electricity when they spin.

TO LEARN MORE

BOOKS

Bowman, Chris. *Dams*. Minneapolis: Bellwether Media, 2019.

Krajnik, Elizabeth. *How a Dam is Built*. New York: Gareth Stevens Publishing, 2020.

Yasuda, Anita. *Exploring Hoover Dam*. Mendota Heights, MN: Focus Readers, 2020.

ONLINE RESOURCES

Visit **www.apexeditions.com** to find links and resources related to this title.

ABOUT THE AUTHOR

Ashley Gish has authored many juvenile nonfiction books. She enjoys learning and sharing information with others. Ashley lives in southern Minnesota with her family.

INDEX

ANSWER KEY:
1. Answers will vary; 2. Answers will vary; 3. B; 4. B; 5. C; 6. A